Chester Martin Schultz

A Rawhide Memoir

Chester M. Schultz
Lieutenant Colonel USAF (Retired)

DEDICATION

This autobiography is dedicated to my family and the men of the United States Air Force who keep America safe and liberty and freedom alive.

CONTENTS

ACKNOWLEDGMENTS

I want to sincerely thank my loving daughter, Laura Nix, who has given me the life blood and will to publish this. She and her family, my closest relations, have been godsends and given hope which has displaced despair. Laura, I love you so much. My loving grandsons and their families have given me hope for the future.

Beginnings

I was the eighth child of a family of ten born to my parents, Felix and Frances Schultz.

During the heart of the depression in the 1930's, all members of the family had a job regardless of how poor the wages were during those years. Since our family consisted of eight not counting my parents my mother devoted most of her time to preparing meals, baking bread and seeing that all members of the family were well fed.

We lived in a middle-to-upper middle class neighborhood. A brother of my dad's, John who lived in Wisconsin, came to Chicago seeking better employment. To accommodate my uncle my dad prepared a room for him in the attic of our home. At the time I was 10 or 12 years old. Therefore, the task of helping my mother was my responsibility. Mother devoted herself in the preparation of meals and I helped her keep the house clean and tidy. We both shopped together. As often as I could I watched her prepare the meals in the kitchen.

I attended James Monroe Elementary School on Schubert Avenue. I was enrolled in a junior high school at Kelvyn Park High School. Studies came easily for me. I never had to take books home because I spent my study hours doing whatever homework was assigned. During my years in school I worked in a fruit store owned by a Jewish man named Louis Borden on Saturdays stocking fruit and delivering orders. Mr. Borden was fair but demanding. Usually on Saturdays customers would ask that their packages be delivered to their homes. It was my chore to see that this was done. I enjoyed doing this because I was often tipped for my services. For this I was paid $3.00/week. In addition I accepted the job of delivering a weekly paper, The Downtown Shopper. For placing the papers in doorway of homes and apartments, I earned $.90/delivery. I was 15 or 16 years old at this time. Once a week sometimes a special would take me out again to deliver. Whenever I had free time I would play softball in the neighborhood school yard with my friends. It depended on the time of year. Sometimes we played touch football.

During my early years my sister Agnes thought someone should learn to play the upright piano that we had. I was nominated. I progressed rapidly and started to take private lessons. My teacher, Mr. Fingerhut, was an outstanding music teacher. He would come to our home and spend an hour reviewing my lesson. After several years I mastered a great number of classical musical pieces. I was called upon to play the piano whenever we had an assembly at school.

I continued my studies at Kelvyn Park High School and graduated in the upper ½ of a class of 400. I graduated in January 1937 at age 18. Mother, Dad, and sisters, Rose and

Agnes, attended the ceremony. In my circle of friends I was the only one who graduated from high school. I enrolled at Wright Junior College and completed two semesters. I had a job at Montgomery Ward & Co. In the mail order facility. They housed everything there that was found in the catalog. I worked in the dinnerware department. Wages were $.25/hr. My fee rose to $.27/hr. Due to my work ethic. I realized there was no future working here. Eight months later I got a job at the Continental Can Company feeding pieces of aluminum into a machine that made cans. I worked the swing shift from 4 PM to midnight. But that too was not an exciting job. My wages were $18-20/week. I was 18 years old.

I had two older brothers, Leo and Henry, who did citizen military training one month/year at Ft. Sheridan. They did this for 4 years being housed in tents and sleeping on the ground by Lake Michigan. Each had attended the summer courses. I remember my brother Henry returning from camp one summer. He was suntanned and in great physical condition and was the picture of health. His last bit of training was with the cavalry and he talked with such enthusiasm. My brothers inspired me to pursue the same training. Upon graduation from this training both were qualified to receive a reserve commission in the U.S. Army. When they took the final physical exam, both were disqualified because they had perforated ear drums. With my parent's permission I must mention that starting in 1935 through 1939 I took advantage of going to Ft. Sheridan attending one month /year with the citizen military training camp. During these months I was taught the basic skills of an Infantry officer. I found it a great experience. I was with young men my age and we shared much together. Graduating from these months of training I was qualified to work for a second lieutenant's commission. There were correspondence extension courses mailed to me in a group of 10 as a series, such as Map Reading, First Aid, Military Justice, Weapons Tactics or Organization of the Army. Each lesson or problem I completed was graded by another instructor for which I received a graded symbol. When these courses were finished, a person appeared before a board of officers and was grilled on all subjects. I was 20 years old when I was in the Army Reserves. It was during this period (1940's) that Congress passed the draft law requiring the selection of young men to serve in the armed services. As a young man unmarried with no dependents and physically qualified, I was sure to be drafted. It was during this time that I made the acquaintance of my future wife. She was a pretty girl, intelligent, came from an excellent family and in comparison, stood head and shoulders above all other girls that I knew.

In 1939 from July through the Fall I went into the Civilian Conservation Corps for 6 months in the state of

Washington at Entiat. My brother Ben was already enrolled and it really changed him. I was sent by train to a camp site in the Wenatchee National Forest as a lumberjack cutting and saving trees using hand saws and axes. These saws were 8 – 10 ft. Long and required two men to operate them. I teamed with a nice person named Stanley Sima who also came from west Chicago. Sometimes we fought forest fires. The work developed my body and I gained weight. In 6 months I weighed 200 lbs. Working in the forest and eating well, I was in great physical shape after 6 months. I learned to appreciate life outdoors and the beauty of the forest in the state of Washington. One time while I was using an ax, the ax slipped and became embedded in my shin. I spent one day in bed after the doctor sewed my leg, but I was so bored I went back to work. Looking back, I realize how exciting it was to experience this great adventure.

Partners in Life

While in the C.C.C. I was writing to my girlfriend, Irene and she wrote to me every day. She was educated having graduated from Lucy Flower Technical High School in Chicago. Here she learned the skills of preparing meals, sewing clothes, and caring for infants being well prepared for a happy marriage. She was witty, lots of fun and had a good personality. She worked hard and was lovable. I knew I had found the girl for me. When I returned to Chicago for weeks we only saw each other on weekends. At these times we would see our friends or take in a movie. Many weekends we would include ballroom dancing. One of our favorite spots was to dance at the famous Aragon Ballroom which featured well known bands. On October 6, 1940 after seeking her father's permission we became engaged celebrating at my parent's home on Central Park. In attendance were Irene's parents, a few of my sisters and other members of her family. It was a joyous occasion. On October 10, 1940 I joined the Army. I was not drafted, but went to the recruiting station at the U.S. Court House in Chicago. I was selected for the Army Air Corps because I had some junior college at Wright Junior College. I was sent to Chanute Field located in Rantoul, Illinois which is about 100 miles south of Chicago. Here as a Private I studied many aircraft maintenance subjects. These courses prepared me to be an aircraft mechanic. Since we only studied five days a week, I was able to get leave and always traveled to Chicago not only to see my girl, Irene, but also to see my parents. I managed to find a fellow soldier who had an automobile and was willing to take passengers with him to Chicago as long as we paid for the gasoline to help defray the expenses. Irene and I would go dancing or take in a movie with friends. We always departed for the base Sunday afternoon. I was there 4-5 months before being sent to Puerto Rico after graduation. When Irene realized I would be leaving in 30 days, she got the wheels in motion and we set a wedding date. There were so many details to be taken care of, nevertheless everything fell into place. It was unbelievable how Irene's sisters organized and made all the preparations for our wedding. Genevieve and Janet contacted our friends and the priest. An orchestra was hired and a large ballroom was reserved. Irene's parents spared no expense to insure that it was perfect. I arranged 30 days of leave and we were married on June 15, 1941 at St. Hyacinth Roman Catholic Church. Since my future father-in-law was treasurer of the Polish American Club, we had a Polish menu at the reception. I t was a wonderful wedding with all our friends and relatives in attendance. I had selected as my best man Bill Domik. He along with other friends made up the wedding party. There were 17 in the wedding party. We took a honeymoon for 3 weeks borrowing my bride's father's 1940 Buick Super. Our first stop was Clinton, Iowa and then we drove through Wisconsin, Minnesota, South Dakota (seeing the Black Hills and Mount Rushmore), Wyoming (seeing Yellowstone National Park)and Montana (seeing where Gen Custer and the 7th Cavalry took its last stand). We saw herds of buffalo. There were no facilities at Mount Rushmore at this time. There were only wooden steps to the top of George Washington's head. In those days there was no such thing as first class motels. We stayed in cabins that were available where the cost varied from $1.50 to $2.00 per night. Usually they provided an electric hot plate so we could warm some soup or other food.   I remember living on Campbell's Chicken Noodle Soup for practically the whole trip. After a leisurely two weeks we returned to Chicago taking a different path of return. But, gosh, what wonderful memories! Upon our return I was scheduled to be in New York to take a transport to Puerto Rico.

Military Service

When I arrived at the Brooklyn Army Base in New York, the Sergeant in charge said the ship was not ready to sail so we were allowed to visit New York City. I spent a week taking the subway into the city taking in all the sights such as the zoo or China town. I boarded the transport ship and after 5 days at sea we finally arrived in San Juan, P.R. From here all the soldiers and airmen were loaded into trucks and taken to their destination. I ended up at Borinquen Field. It was still under construction by civilian engineers. Quarters were under construction for married officers and families as well as senior NCO's. In addition barracks were being built to accommodate the enlisted personnel. Until such time as they were built and ready to be occupied, we lived in tents. Puerto Rico was still infested with mosquitos that carried malaria so we slept under netting to avoid the disease. I settled into a routine of going to the flight line and assisting others in the maintenance of B-18 aircraft. I enjoyed working with seasoned specialists and gained a lot of knowledge about the aircraft. This was a Douglas medium bomber powered by 2 reciprocating engines. It was a sturdy aircraft and was in constant use. These aircraft were assigned to the 40th Bomb Group. Each squadron that composed the group was assigned their own aircraft. I was in the 44th Bomb Squadron. From time to time I was a crew member and flew training missions. About this time I was promoted to Sergeant. Prior to Pearl Harbor, theb-18's were used primarily for training pilots. However, after the bombing of Pearl Harbor they were used to patrol the Caribbean Sea and insuring the protection of the Panama Canal.

In October or November 1941 our barracks were completed and we moved into our new quarters. They were well made, had shower facilities and a series of sinks where a person could shave and complete his grooming. On December 7, 1941 Japan bombed Pearl Harbor and we were devastated. Two days after that Germany declared war against the U.S. By this time I had been notified that I was appointed a 2nd Lieutenant in the Infantry Reserves. One day after Pearl Harbor was attacked; a German submarine appeared off the coast of Puerto Rico and shelled a petroleum complex. There wasn't much publicity reported by the authorities as they didn't want much information released as to how successful the attack was. The biggest effect was the chaos it created. No one knew what to do. We had to defend the base. Many men threw mattresses over the banister to protect themselves from any shelling. Aircraft raced down the runway with limited crews and no bombs on board. Had the submarine commander sent a squad of personnel ashore with their automatic weapons, they could have easily taken over the base and destroyed the facilities. To this day it has been referred to as the Battle of Borinquen. The island then declared a strict blackout and the base went on alert. Finally some semblance of order was established. Our B-18 aircraft were sent to search the sea for enemy submarines which were sinking allied transports carrying lend lease supplies to Great Britain. To my knowledge none were ever seen. From that day forward, aircraft patrolled the seas and devoted much effort to protecting the Panama Canal.

On April 1, 1942 I received orders calling me to active duty as a 2nd Lieutenant. I left Borinquen A.B. and was flown to another base at Ponce. Upon arrival I was assigned as assistant Base Engineering officer under Capt. William Pumplin, a veteran who had served as an enlisted man but was highly qualified as a technical engineer. My education now started. This organization was staffed with highly trained technical personnel. I learned a lot and the Captain was like a father to me. I stayed in this assignment until I was sent to help Capt. Dumont, Squadron Leader of the 63rd Maintenance Squadron. Unfortunately he and a full load of passengers were killed in an airplane accident. I then became Squadron Leader. In addition to those duties the headquarters gave me additional duties to perform such as investigating officer in reference to crimes, defense counsel, specialty court, helping to inventory the base PX and many others which kept me very busy. I acquired a great deal of experience in squadron activities and airmen. This was only true because of the shortage of commissioned officers. After one year I was promoted to First Lieutenant. Lt. Richard Willer, our base commander did an outstanding job of seeing that the base ran smoothly. My assignments varied based upon needs. I finally ended up as Base Engineering officer prior to my departure for the U.S.A. mainland after 2 ½ years in the Fall of 1943. Upon completion of my assignment in Base Engineering, I was put in command of the Headquarters Squadron. The Squadron duty was more interesting. I had a great First Sergeant who was familiar with all of the details of running a smooth organization. One of the things of which I became aware was the lack of security. I managed to procure Garand rifles and ammunition. I devoted much of my time in training and preparing the base in event of an enemy landing party. While I was stationed at Ponce I was sent to Ft. Buchanan in San Juan to the Transportation Course where I learned to drive a 2 ton truck and a motor cycle and maintain them.

To recap some of the officers that I became acquainted with and helped run the base were: Maj Pop May, Capt. Art lacrown, Maj. Ben Forbes, W.O. Riser, Capt. Art Colu, Capt. William Dahn, Capt. William Pumplin, Capt. Bill Silance. These were but a few of the officers that ran the base efficiently.

Returning to mainland I was assigned to the Miami Redistribution Center for processing and further assignment. One of my sergeants Art Nikas who was with me at Borinquen applied for OCS and was a candidate while I was in Miami. Arthur's wife Betty came to Miami and joined Irene whom I brought to Miami after I arrived in the states. After a month of processing and awaiting an assignment, I received orders to Hill A.F.B. in Utah. Upon arrival at Hill Field, I was assigned to the class O1 warehouse. Here I was an assistant to Lt. Saul Schwartz. This kept me busy and I really learned much about warehouse and supplies. My superior was Col. William Shields, an old reserve officer but very much qualified. Before Col Shields sent me from Hill AFB Utah to Denver CO to assume command of the 837th Special Depot, Irene became pregnant with our daughter. While in Denver she carried the baby well. After some months I was put in charge of the Stock Control Branch. In the meantime the Air Force promoted me to Captain. I stayed in this position until tagged to take over the 837th Support Depot in Denver, CO. My task was to dispose of all material in the 5 warehouses we had under our jurisdiction. The civilians were very qualified and I gained two officers and Capt. Charles Harris who was assigned to me primarily to be close to Fitzsimmons General Hospital. Capt. Harris, while a prisoner of the Germans, had been mistreated and developed ulcers on his legs which required medical attention. Lt. Dudley Abbott was also with me and handled the contracting end of our business to dispose of the Air Force items in the warehouse. When my assignment was completed and I closed the depot, we returned to Hill AFB. After I returned to Hill AFB I was sent to Ft. Leavenworth, KS for Army Command and General Staff school for 5 months planning for the invasion of Japan tactically in 1945. Irene was very pregnant and when we returned to Utah, the base hospital at Hill AFB was unable to care for expectant mothers. Therefore, we made arrangements for Irene to be under the care of Dr. Whirit, an outstanding OB/GYN specialist. Our daughter was born at Holy Cross Hospital in Salt Lake City, Utah on March 21, 1947. Mother and daughter came through the ordeal with flying colors. I was so proud of Irene and the baby. We named her Laura Jeanne. A great friend of ours, Peter Lonetto, who served with me in Puerto Rico, was on hand to help with the celebration. While at Hill A.F.B. I had several temporary duty assignments and was sent as a student to the Air Force Tactical School at Panama City, Florida in 1947. Once again I learned much about being a good officer.

This period of my life goes back to the 1950's when the Cold War was at its height. The Soviet Union never did demobilize their Army and Air Force after WWII. They continued to use their forces as a threat to the West. To counter this threat the United States developed the Strategic

Air Force commanded by General Curtis Lemay. Gen Lemay demanded that his bombers be ready to counteract any threat by being 100% in readiness. In the meantime I was sent to Wright Field to Supply Directorate – Bldg. 262. Large headquarters for Air Depot. There was a four star general and my general in command. My assignment was to be the deputy chief of supply directorate to check to see how it was maintained. A crew of experts traveled to different organizations and inspected the facilities then gave a briefing and made a report. I was soon pushed up in front with Col Kauffman. The invasion of South Korea was in 1950. The United States was fighting the Chinese and North Koreans. The general sent me to New York City to the office of the quartermaster. Gen Hoyt Vandenburg, a West Point graduate and the Chief of Staff of the Air Force, contacted Sears and Roebuck Co to acquire supplies needed for the action in Korea. Sam Epstein and I bought kitchen and other equipment to support the Korean War. While in New York Sam contracted the flu and I was assigned to escort Gen Chidlaw to the meeting of the representatives of the industries. At this time Col Lester Light telephoned me and told me that I was promoted to Major. Also while I was there I received a telephone call from the manufacturer of the AF blue uniforms who said that they could not meet the threads per inch specification for the cloth for the uniforms and wished to receive approval for a deviation from this requirement. I authorized the deviation by letter. When the New York assignment was over, Gen Vandenburg promoted Sam Epstein to Colonel in the AF Reserves. I returned to Wright Field assigned to Area Activities.

Returning to Hill A.F.B. I was given a number of assignments. I was assigned to the Supply Directorate at the Ogden AMC at Hill AFB Utah. I was made chief of Stock Control. My sole responsibility was to ensure that the aircraft were manned and armed. My office consisted of 90 civilians who kept track of the supplies. Records were maintained on Kardex cards in cabinets. Each employee had sole responsibility for the items under their control. I had two senior civilian employees, two W.A.F.s, one warrant officer and two rated Captains under me whose purpose was to expedite items that were required to maintain the aircraft. The two flying officers made a unit referred to as AOCP or aircraft out of commission. We were in competition with other depots. Because the aircraft were out of commission due to lack of parts, one Friday night after work Capt Cavanaugh and I flew to Middletown Air Materiel Area (MAMA), in Middletown, PA in an A-26 to pick up parts. Stripped of its armament it was repudiated to cruise between 300 – 400 mph, the A-26 was a fast light weight bomber at Hill AFB, Utah. The aircraft was powered by two Pratt and Whitney engines which made a lot of noise. I could not carry on a conversation with Capt. Cavanaugh. The sergeant who was crew chief went to sleep in the nose of the plane as soon as we were airborne. I curled up and dozed off also. It was a beautiful night. The controls were on one side only. I was awakened by the loud noise of the engines. The engines were full throttle and we were headed straight for the ground. I glanced at Capt. Cavanaugh and he too had dozed off apparently. I shouted with all my strength, "Charlie! Charlie!" He sluggishly pulled back on the controls and brought the aircraft out of the dive. When we landed at our first stop, Offut AFB in Nebraska to refuel and buy coffee, leaves and debris were found on the undercarriage of the plane by two civilians who readied the plane. We kept the windows open for the rest of the flight even though it was very cold. We flew on to MAMA, picked up our supplies that were waiting for us and returned to Ogden without further incident. Later I thought, "God happens to be our co-pilot! I will save Capt. Schultz's life. He will be required to care for his wife in time when she develops Alzheimer disease. " And so it was. Another time I was given an opportunity to fly to Chicago and see the family for several days. The aircraft from Hill AFB to Chicago was a C-47, a two engine cargo aircraft. They were transporting people from that area to places beyond. After spending several days with family we were returning to Hill AFB when the plane filled with gasoline fumes. We lost an engine and had to make an emergency landing at Warren AFB in Wyoming. As soon as we touched down five enlisted airmen and I jumped out of the plane and rolled when we hit the ground. I injured my left leg in the fall. We stayed long enough for them to fix the airplane and we returned to Hill AFB. Once again God spared my life.

We left Hill AFB and I was assigned to Wright Patterson AFB. From there I was sent to Toronto, Canada for two years. I wrote to say that two years would be a waste of time and one year was all that was needed. I was assigned to Sqdrn. Ldr. E.E. Smith of the RCAF. I was supervisor in charge of the shipping and packing department of supplies to all of their bases. Sgt. Spurgen worked under me. As we received requisitions for supplies, we would fill the orders. In many cases we had to place these supplies in storage waiting for the weather to clear for delivery to the bases. When I left Toronto I was assigned WPAFB as chief of equipage. We would have equipment such as parachutes shipped directly from the manufacturer to the base where the aircraft needed them. We lived in Fairborn and our son Philip Jon was born on May 28, 1953. While Phil was a baby we went to England by ship, the America, in February 1954. In England we lived in Shirley, Croyden and I worked for PROV MAAG K in London.

During our stay in London my assignment was at Grosvenor House. With other U.S. Air Force officers I was to arrange for the smooth transfer of B-29 aircraft to the Royal

Air Force. We were to insure that with the transfer of the aircraft, there were enough spare parts and equipment given so that the aircraft was operational without further support from the United States. My office consisted of the following officers: Robert Smith, Jim Kelly, Herbert Brothers and Warren Harding. Each person had a specific role in the transfer of the aircraft. Also included in the office was a civilian employee named Robert Kidde. We had four non-commissioned enlisted men to do the paper work – filing etc. Robert Kidde apparently received his typing and office training in high school. During WW II he served under a senior general performing office duties. When the war ended he remained in Europe finally drifting to the American Embassy. Here he was employed as a clerk. He was assigned to our office for employment.

The next phase involves Lord Audley. A graduate of the best schools in England and truly an English gentleman, he was married to Sarah Churchill, Winston Churchill's daughter. After a number of years their marriage fell apart. The courts awarded Sarah Churchill Lord Audley's estates, land and other valuable property. Thus for all intents and purposes he was practically penniless. How he became friendly with Mr. Kidde, we don't know but nevertheless they became inseparable. With Mr. Kidde's influence Lord Audley was employed by the U.S. government. He was entitled to all the privileges, i.e. commissary and other facilities. He apparently financed a small shop where Lord Audley became involved in the sale of crystal ware. To foster interest and sale of the crystal he employed an artist from Paris, France to paint the ballerinas on the crystal glasses. He had two complete sets made. When the artist finished painting these glasses of the dancers from the Sadler Wells Ballet, he had a showing. It was then that Irene and I attended this affair and really became friendly with Lord Audley. After this publicity in London newspapers, they decided to visit America and present a complete set to the Art Institute in New York City. Lord Audley once again received a great deal of publicity. When all the publicity finally died down, Mr. Kidde and Lord Audley ventured to California where Mr. Kidde's parents resided. Once again a great deal of interest and publicity was generated. The friends and family of Mr. Kidde wined and dined them. After several weeks they decided it was time to return to England. Lord Audley took on his role as a member of the House of Lords and from all indicators became a very popular member of the House. He once again became accepted into the circle of high society of his breeding. Then we heard that he married a rich widow regaining his rightful status as a member of his society. Thus ends the saga of Lord Audley. Incidentally, a street adjacent to the American embassy bears his name.

There was another story that ended in London while we

were stationed there. When Hitler invaded Poland on September 1, 1939, the first waves of German Stuka bombers destroyed Warsaw's newspaper building. This facility belonged to Mr. Velesky, a multimillionaire who was educated at the best European universities. He was also a member of the Polish parliament. Mr. Velesky managed to escape with his life and fled to England as a refugee. His wife, however, remained in Poland and became involved in the Polish underground. His only son who was a member of the Polish Air Force flew his plane to England and became involved with the Royal Air Force. During the Battle of Britain he lost his life combating the German onslaught. In time word was received that Mrs. Velesky was apprehended by the Nazis. Arrested and placed in a prison camp she was later put to death in the gas chambers.

Since my father-in-law was associated with Polish organizations in the United States, he was contacted to encourage Mr. Velesky to immigrate to the USA. Because of my contacts at the American embassy in London, I was asked to intercede and arrange for a visa. A city in Pennsylvania was seeking just the right person to run their town's Polish newspaper. Irene and I managed to make contact with Mr. Velesky. What a delight he was! He was a true aristocrat and a gentleman of the highest order. When he met Irene he would kiss her hand as was customary with a person of this class. It was a pleasure to be with him. Although I had difficulty with his speech, Irene managed to carry on a conversation with him. For all intents and purposes he escaped to England without any funds. At this time in England he was working at night in an ice cream factory. Consequently, he was able to meet with us during the day. He had a visa to immigrate to America. However, his health exam showed he had a spot on his lung. Therefore, he was refused entrance in the United States until this spot disappeared. In the meantime, his visa expired so we worked to have it reinstated. While we were waiting with him we treated him to a movie at the Odeum cinema at Hyde Park. He was excited and thrilled at the beauty of the United States. At this point his health exam was passed and all seemed well for him to leave for America. Then he was contacted by a person who informed him of a relative that had survived the war and was alive in Poland. As a result he elected to return to Poland. Irene and I were scheduled to return to the U.S. so we lost track of him in Poland. Word reached us, however, that some months later he developed pneumonia and died. Thus ends the saga of Mr. Velesky.

After three years in England, we returned home on the steamship the United States in April 1956. I was assigned to Stoney Brook AFS, MA as a squadron commander. Stoney Brook AFS was a special depot where the hydrogen bombs were stored and available to be loaded on the B-52's stationed at Westover AFB in MA. At this time the Soviet

Union and the United States were not communicating and threatening to bomb each other during the Cold War. The B-52's were always on alert as they were part of the Strategic Air Command under Gen Curtis Lemay. As squadron commander I was on alert either by telephone or standby alert.

Upon completion of my three year tour I received orders to go to South Korea and was authorized to have my family accompany me. Upon arrival in South Korea I was assigned to a special office under the supervision of the South Korean Secretary of Defense. I was given the assignment of ascertaining whether there were facilities in South Korea available to manufacture shoes and boots for their military forces. To assist me in this project a South Korean officer, Capt. Oh, of the ROK Navy was assigned to me. He was assigned because he could speak some English. As a team we searched the area of northern South Korea for appropriate facilities that would be able to meet the manufacturing requirements. Unable to find what was needed, he and I boarded a train and went to the southern part of South Korea to explore that area and ascertain if there were any facilities that could meet the manufacturing requirements. By interviewing people in that area we stumbled upon an elderly woman who remembered some activity that was happening in the back of a farmer's field. Capt. Oh and I removed our shoes, rolled up our pants and waded through the rice paddies. After some distance we found what we were searching for. There was a complete facility that had been established by the West German government under the auspices of United States Overseas Mission (USOM). Upon returning to Seoul we made a verbal report and showed pictures to the ROK Defense minister. The Minister was so elated that he promoted Capt. Oh to Commodore and I was decorated for my role in this project.

In as much as I had been assigned to South Korea as a hardship tour, I was given preferential choice for my next tour of duty. I opted for an assignment to Hawaii and was sent to Hickam AFB. Here I was Chief of Supply and Services at Hickam AFB. I spent two years at this assignment and thoroughly enjoyed my association with the officers and civilians under me. After two years I was sent to the mainland on the ship the Lurline. The family drove across country to the Washington, DC area where I was assigned to the Defense Supply Agency in Alexandria, VA. This Agency's mission was premier in supporting the Southeast Asia military operations. After spending three years at this assignment, I retired from the AF with 30 years of service on August 1, 1967 receiving the AF Commendation Service medal.

ABOUT THE AUTHOR

Chester Martin Schultz now lives in Peoria, Arizona. His thirty year career in the United States Air Force included overseas assignments in Puerto Rico, the United Kingdom, Canada, and Republic of Korea in addition to stateside tours in Utah, Colorado, Massachusetts, Ohio, Alabama, Florida and Virginia. His Logistic and Supply responsibilities for leather and woolen goods during his Air Force assignments earned him the call sign of Rawhide. He holds a Bachelor of

Science degree from the University of Maryland and a Master of Arts degree from the George Washington University. He and his wife, Irene, enjoyed a sixty-nine year marriage adventure before she passed away in 2010.

www.ingramcontent.com/pod-product-compliance
Lightning Source LLC
Chambersburg PA
CBHW060554030426
42337CB00019B/3549